EVANSTON PUBLIC LIBRARY

W9-AOM-685

x551.5 Kahl.J

Kahl, Jonathan D.

Weatherwise : learning
about the weather /
c1992.

HOLIDAY BOOK FUND

HOLIDAY BOOK FUND

A Gift
From

MARY CAROL BUCHOLTZ

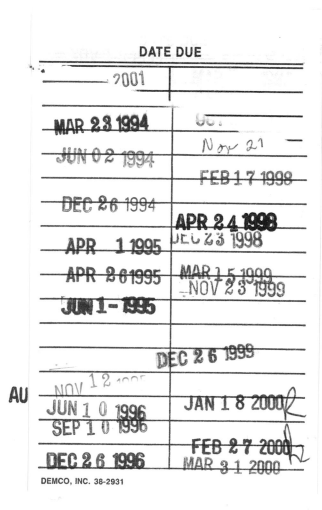

DATE DUE

2001	
MAR 2 3 1994	OCT
JUN 0 2 1994	Nov 21
	FEB 1 7 1998
DEC 2 6 1994	
	APR 2 4 1998
APR 1 1995	DEC 2 3 1998
APR 2 6 1995	MAR 1 5 1999
JUN 1 - 1995	NOV 2 3 1999
	DEC 2 6 1999
AU NOV 1 2 1995	
JUN 1 0 1996	JAN 1 8 2000
SEP 1 0 1996	
DEC 2 6 1996	FEB 2 7 2000
	MAR 3 1 2000

DEMCO, INC. 38-2931

WEATHERWISE

For Joey

All words printed in **bold** are explained in the glossary that begins on page 60.

Copyright © 1992 Lerner Publications Company

All rights reserved. International copyright secured. No part of this book may be reproduced or transmitted in any form or by any means, electronic or mechanical, including photocopying and recording, or by any information storage or retrieval system, without permission in writing from the publisher, except for the inclusion of brief quotations in an acknowledged review.

Library of Congress Cataloging-in-Publication Data

Kahl, Jonathan D.
    Weatherwise: learning about the weather / Jonathan D. Kahl.
        p.   cm. — (How's the weather?)
    Includes index.
    Summary: Discusses many aspects of weather, including climate and the seasons, wind, humidity, clouds, rain, and weather forecasting.
    ISBN 0-8225-2525-9
    1. Weather — Juvenile literature. [1. Weather.] I. Title.
II. Title: Weatherwise. III. Series: Kahl, Jonathan D. How's the weather?
QC981.3.K34   1991   91-2015
551.6 — dc20   CIP
                                                                         AC

Manufactured in the United States of America

1 2 3 4 5 6 7 8 9 10 01 00 99 98 97 96 95 94 93 92

WEATHERWISE

LEARNING ABOUT THE WEATHER

by Jonathan D. Kahl

Lerner Publications Company / Minneapolis

EVANSTON PUBLIC LIBRARY
CHILDREN'S DEPARTMENT
1703 ORRINGTON AVENUE
EVANSTON, ILLINOIS 60201

CONTENTS

INTRODUCTION

The weather is a favorite subject of conversation for just about everybody. "How was the weather during your vacation?" "I hope the sky clears up for our picnic this afternoon." "It's cold outside—be sure to bring a sweater." These are just a few of the remarks people often make about the weather.

Talking about the weather is so natural that most of us do it without even thinking: "Nice day, isn't it?" We have many sayings that use weather terminology, for example: "That homework assignment was a breeze," and "I'll take a rain check." Some comedians like to make jokes about the weather: "Everybody talks about the weather, but nobody does anything about it."

Benjamin Franklin was one of the first **meteorologists**, the people who study and predict the weather. Over two hundred years ago he wrote, "Some people are weatherwise, but most are otherwise." This observation is quite true. Almost everybody knows a little bit about the weather, but few people are truly "weatherwise."

What is the weather, anyway? Meteorologists will tell you that weather is the condition of the **atmosphere**, or the air, at a specific

6

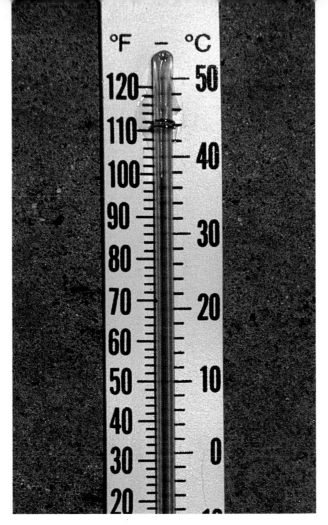

A thermometer uses two different scales to measure temperature: Fahrenheit and Celsius. On the Fahrenheit scale, which is commonly used in the United States, the temperature at which water freezes is 32°, and the point at which it boils is 212°. The Celsius scale is widely used outside of the United States. On the Celsius scale, water freezes at 0° and boils at 100°.

time and place. The weather often changes from day to day. A meteorologist might predict hot, dry weather for your town one day, and rain the next.

Another term often used by meteorologists is **climate**, which refers to the most typical weather conditions for a region on Earth. Weather and climate are complex topics. But this book will help you better understand what causes different weather conditions in different places on Earth, and what causes the weather to change.

1

EARTH AND
THE ATMOSPHERE

Air is strange stuff. You can't grab onto it, yet it is strong enough to blow you off your feet. You can't feel air, even though it is pressing down on you with a weight of thousands of pounds. You can't see air, but you can see rain and snow falling through it. You can't hear air, but sometimes you can listen to the howl of the wind and the crashing of thunder. We hardly ever think about it, but we could not live more than a few minutes without air.

When someone mentions the atmosphere (or the air), people usually think about the weather. We wonder about the temperature, about whether or not it will rain, or about the strength of the wind. People don't often realize how important the air is to our health and well-being.

The atmosphere is a mixture of many invisible gases. Over three-fourths of the atmosphere is made up of *nitrogen*, a gas that enriches the soil and helps plants grow. About one-fifth of the atmosphere is made up of *oxygen*. All animals, including humans, breathe oxygen—we couldn't live without it. Nitrogen and oxygen together account for almost 99 percent of the atmosphere. Other

Sunlight, air, and water are the important ingredients that combine to make the weather on Earth.

gases are present in smaller amounts, but without them life would be absolutely impossible. These other ingredients include *ozone*, which shields us from the Sun's harmful **ultraviolet radiation**, and *carbon dioxide*, a gas that plants need to breathe.

LAYERS OF THE ATMOSPHERE

The atmosphere is divided into several different layers. The layer closest to the Earth's surface is called the troposphere. The name comes from the Greek word *tropos,* which means "change" and refers to the moving winds and changing weather near the ground. Most people spend all of their lives in the troposphere.

Above the troposphere we find the stratosphere, which includes the "ozone layer." Above the stratosphere is the mesosphere, and finally the thermosphere.

The atmosphere becomes thinner the higher you go. That is, there is less gas, including oxygen, contained there. There is no distinct upper boundary to the atmosphere—the air at the top of the thermosphere is so thin that it slowly blends into space.

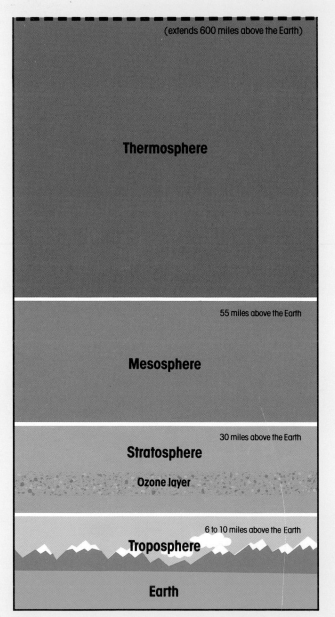

(extends 600 miles above the Earth)

Thermosphere

55 miles above the Earth

Mesosphere

30 miles above the Earth

Stratosphere

Ozone layer

6 to 10 miles above the Earth

Troposphere

Earth

THE WATER CYCLE
After rainwater falls on land, it might travel—by way of rivers, streams, and waterfalls—back to the ocean. From there, the water evaporates and enters the atmosphere once more.

Perhaps the most important minor ingredient of the atmosphere is **water vapor**. Water vapor is created when liquid water heats up and changes into a gas. This process is called **evaporation**. You can create water vapor simply by heating a pot of water on the stove.

Most of the water vapor in the air is produced when the Sun's heat evaporates water at the surface of the oceans. This water vapor is carried long distances by the wind. The vapor gathers together, forming clouds, and eventually the water returns to the land, rivers, and oceans in the form of rain and snow. This complete process, called the **water cycle**, guarantees a constant supply of water vapor for the atmosphere.

The entire atmosphere, with all of its ingredients, is over 600 miles (965 kilometers) deep. This may sound pretty thick, but actually the atmosphere is quite thin. If the Earth were compared to the size of an apple, the atmosphere would be thinner than the apple's skin.

The pressure inside airplanes is controlled so that people feel comfortable at high elevations—where the air pressure is low. Sometimes you feel your ears plug up or "pop" on an airplane trip. You feel uncomfortable because your body is adjusting to the changing pressure.

The atmosphere presses down on us with a weight of more than 2,000 pounds (908 kilograms) for every square foot of the Earth's surface. Imagine carrying 2,000 pounds on your shoulders—we all do it every minute of the day. The weight of the air above us is called **air pressure**. (The air pressure doesn't crush you because the air all around you supports the weight of the air from above.)

The higher you go into the atmosphere, the lower the air pressure becomes. This is because as you go higher, there is more air below you and less air above to press down on you.

The air is also "thinner" at high elevations. Near the ground, the gas **molecules** in the air are numerous and packed closely together by the great pressure of the atmosphere. But as you go higher, pressure decreases, and the gas molecules, including oxygen, become more scattered. The air is so thin at the tops of tall mountains that mountain climbers traveling above 10,000 feet (3,048 meters) sometimes have to wear oxygen masks in order to breathe.

Sunlight and Energy

Our bodies need energy for every activity we do. When we run out of energy, we replenish it by eating and resting. The atmosphere needs energy too. Where does the air find the strength to create howling winds, blinding rains, and raging blizzards? Most of this energy comes from the Sun.

SUNBATHERS BEWARE!

Most of the atmosphere's ozone is located in the stratosphere. Ozone is a very important gas, because it prevents many of the Sun's harmful ultraviolet rays from reaching the ground. The Earth's ozone shield has thinned recently, and many people are concerned about the health risks this might pose. Ultraviolet rays can cause skin cancer in people and can kill plants and animals.

Many scientists believe that gases used in aerosol spray cans, refrigerators, and air conditioners may be causing the deterioration of the ozone layer.

If you spend time in the Sun, be sure to wear sunglasses and protective sunscreen.

Since the atmosphere is cold at high elevations, you can see snow on tall mountains—even in summer.

The temperature at the surface of the Sun is over 10,000° F (5,582° C). The Sun spreads enormous amounts of heat and light, or solar energy, out into space in every direction. Even though the Sun is over 90 million miles (145 million km) away, some of this energy reaches the Earth. The Sun's energy travels at the speed of light—so fast that it takes only eight minutes for the solar energy to reach the Earth.

Strangely enough, most of the Sun's heat passes right through the atmosphere without heating it at all. Instead, the heat goes straight to the land and oceans, warming them up. The Earth holds the heat and slowly sends it back into the atmosphere.

Have you ever wondered why you often see snow on a mountaintop, even in summer? This occurs because the higher you go into the atmosphere, the farther you are from the stored heat of the Earth and oceans, and the colder the air becomes.

During the day, the Sun warms the Earth, the Earth heats the atmosphere, and the air feels warmer. At night, when the Sun isn't shining on your side of the planet, the Earth cools, and the air cools with it.

THE GREENHOUSE EFFECT

The heating of the atmosphere is similar to the heating of a greenhouse. The glass roof on a greenhouse allows solar energy to pass through, where it is absorbed by the plants inside. The plants and soil warm up and send "Earth energy" back toward the glass roof. But the glass blocks the passage of this type of heat. In this way, the greenhouse stays warm.

Some of the gases in the atmosphere act like glass in a greenhouse. They allow solar energy to pass through, but they prevent Earth energy from escaping. Thus the heat of the Sun is trapped, and the Earth stays warm.

Temperatures around the Earth have increased over the last century, and there is much debate about the cause. A lot of gases enter the atmosphere when people burn fuels such as coal, oil, and wood. Some scientists believe that these gases have magnified the greenhouse effect, trapped more heat near the Earth, and caused global temperatures to rise. Other scientists think global warming may be due to natural changes in climates on Earth.

AURORAS

An aurora is a dazzling display of colored lights occurring more than 100 miles (160 km) above the ground. These lights are given off when electrically charged particles from the Sun strike the Earth's atmosphere. The particles travel toward the North and South poles, hit other charged particles in the atmosphere, and begin to glow and flicker. Auroras are only visible at night.

In the Northern Hemisphere, this light show is called the aurora borealis, or the northern lights. In the Southern Hemisphere, people see the aurora australis, or the southern lights. Auroras are easiest to see at high latitudes—near the North and South poles. Occasionally, however, the northern lights can be seen as far south as the United States.

Rotation and Revolution

We have seen that the Sun's energy is responsible for warm temperatures during the day and cool temperatures at night. But we're getting ahead of ourselves—we haven't yet discussed what causes day and night. The answer, of course, is the circular motion of the Earth itself.

An object can turn in two ways: around itself or around something else. Try it for yourself. First stand up and turn around several times without moving anywhere. This type of motion is called **rotation**. Now, if you're not too dizzy, go outside and walk in a circle around your house. This type of motion is called **revolution**.

The Earth is in constant motion. It rotates around its **axis**—an imaginary line from the North Pole to the South Pole, straight through the center of the Earth—once every 24 hours. It's no coincidence that 24 hours is exactly the length of one day. In fact, this is precisely the definition of a day: the amount of time it takes for the Earth to finish one complete rotation around its axis.

During the daytime, the place where you live on Earth is facing the Sun, which gives you light and heat. Nighttime occurs when the rotation of the Earth takes you away from the Sun, where you face the darkness of outer space.

At the same time the Earth is rotating around its axis, it's also revolving around the Sun. To get an idea of what this is like, try walking in a circle around the outside of your house, rotating around and around at the same time (you'll probably get dizzy again). If we imagine that you are the Earth and your house is the Sun, it will take you one year to revolve around your house. In that time, you'll rotate 365 times—one time for each day.

Now we know exactly what a year is: the amount of time it takes the Earth to finish one complete revolution around the Sun. In that time, the Earth will have traveled 585 million miles (941 million km) through space—more than 1.6 million miles (2.6 million km) each day.

The Changing Seasons

The contrast in temperature between day and night is one of the most important features of the weather. Another important feature is the difference in temperature between the seasons: winter, spring, summer, and fall. Like the change between day and night, the changing seasons are also due to the circular motion of the Earth. But it's not the Earth's rotation that creates the seasons. The Earth's revolution causes the seasons to change.

Revolution isn't the whole story, though. The Earth's axis also plays a crucial role. Instead of pointing straight up and down, the Earth's axis is tilted at an angle of exactly 23½ degrees. The tilt of the Earth doesn't change as the planet circles the Sun.

The upper half of the Earth (the Northern Hemisphere) tilts toward the Sun in summer, but leans away from the Sun in the winter. In summer we have long hours of daylight and warm temperatures. The Sun appears to be high in the sky.

During winter, when your region on the Earth is tipped away from the Sun, the days are short and cold, and the Sun is low in the sky. Meanwhile, when it is winter in the Northern Hemisphere, it is summer in the Southern Hemisphere. So, while people in the United States are sipping hot chocolate and trying to stay warm, Australians may be basking in the hot Sun!

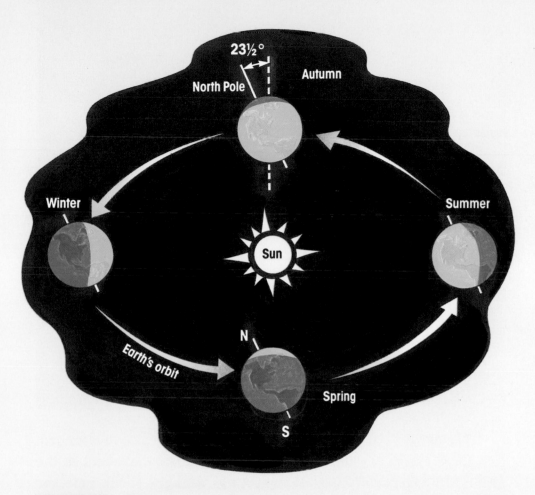

Earth's orbit

THE SEASONS

The Earth is tilted at an angle of 23½ degrees in relation to its path around the Sun. The Northern Hemisphere will tilt away from the Sun during part of the year (winter) and toward the Sun during another part of the year (summer).

When it is summer in the Northern Hemisphere, there are long hours of daylight and warm temperatures. The farther north you go, the more hours of sunlight you receive each day. At the North Pole, the Sun doesn't set at all during the summer, because the pole points toward the Sun, every hour of the day.

Sunset is the time when your region on Earth spins away from the Sun and begins to face the darkness of outer space.

The climates of different parts of the world are also determined, to a large extent, by the amount of solar energy that reaches the ground (or the ocean) in each area. Areas near the North Pole, for instance, receive very little heat from the Sun. The region has a polar climate with cold weather all year round. Farther south is the temperate zone, where temperatures are high in summer and low in winter. Still farther south we find the tropics, near the equator. Temperatures are always high in the tropics because the equator never tilts away from the Sun. The equator always receives plenty of direct sunlight.

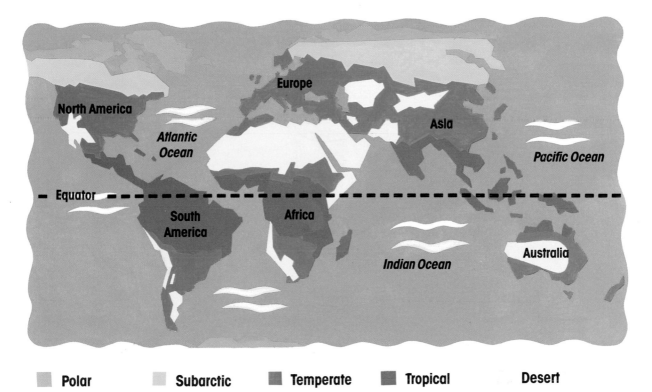

Polar   Subarctic   Temperate   Tropical   Desert

CLIMATE ZONES

Five distinct climate zones are found on Earth. *Polar* climates, the coldest on Earth, occur near the North and South poles. *Subarctic* climates feature light snow, long cold winters, and cool summers. *Temperate* climates are characterized by warm summers, cold winters, and abundant rain and snow. *Desert* climates are hot and dry during most of the year, and *tropical* climates, near the equator, are warm and wet almost all year round.

Many things influence climate, including the amount of sunlight, wind, and moisture that a region receives, geographic features such as mountains, oceans, and rivers, and the kind of soil and plant life found on the land itself.

2

WATER AND THE WEATHER

We mentioned earlier that water vapor (water in gas form) is one of the most important ingredients of the air. Water vapor gets into the air through the constant evaporation of water at the surface of the oceans.

The amount of water vapor in the air is called **humidity.** Meteorologists usually report humidity as a percentage. When the humidity is 100 percent, the air contains all the water vapor that it can hold. Cold air cannot hold as much water vapor as warm air can, which is why your skin often feels dry in the winter.

Hot days in areas with high humidity can make us feel sticky. In the southeastern United States, for example, people sometimes complain that the air feels thick, or muggy. Much of the discomfort people feel on hot, humid days is caused by the humidity rather than the heat. A hot day in the desert, on the other hand, can be quite comfortable. Because deserts are very dry, the humidity is usually low, and the air doesn't feel so thick and stuffy.

Just as liquid water turns to gas when it is heated, water vapor in the air becomes liquid again when it cools. This process is

Frost forms, just like dew, when water vapor condenses on a cool night. If it's cold enough, the water droplets freeze, forming frost.

known as **condensation**, and it is easy to observe in the early morning after a clear, calm night. When air cools during the night, some of the water vapor condenses and forms *dew* — small specks of water that cling to blades of grass, leaves, and other objects.

Condensation is also important for the creation of another familiar weather feature — clouds.

Clouds

Clouds have fascinated people for thousands of years. From the thin, wispy horsetail clouds in a deep blue sky, to the bright, towering storm clouds that look like giant heads of cauliflower, clouds are one of the most beautiful and exciting aspects of the weather. Being able to identify the many different kinds of clouds will help you to understand and — better yet — to predict the weather!

A cloud is a collection of water droplets (or sometimes ice crystals) floating in the air. You'll remember that water vapor is an invisible gas, just like the other ingredients of the air. But the water in clouds is different. First of all, cloud water is not vapor at all— it's usually liquid water. The second difference is one you already know: clouds are not invisible!

The water in clouds comes from water vapor in the air. When air cools, the water vapor condenses into millions and millions of tiny liquid water droplets. The result is a cloud. It doesn't take all that much water to make a cloud. A small cloud the size of your house might contain only a few gallons of water. The cloud droplets usually form around tiny particles in the air called **condensation nuclei.** Some of the most common condensation nuclei are particles of dust, smoke, and salt from ocean spray.

Since temperatures are low at high elevations, water vapor cools and clouds sometimes form when air rises. For example, clouds often form when air flows over a high hill or a mountain.

Clouds are classified by their shape and also by their height above the ground. There are three major types of clouds: *cumulus*, *stratus*, and *cirrus*. Cumulus clouds form less than a mile (1.6 km) above the ground. These are the puffy, white clouds that are commonly seen on a summer afternoon. Cumulus clouds are usually flat on the bottom but oddly shaped on the sides and top. An enjoyable activity for cloud-watchers of all ages is to observe how cumulus clouds form, grow, and disappear. All you need is a little patience (you'll have to sit for at least half an hour) and maybe a blanket. As you watch the clouds, notice how no two are alike. Some clouds may remind you of faces, animals, or other objects—

Altocumulus clouds fill the daytime sky.

which is strange when you remember that clouds are all a collection of tiny water drops!

Cumulus clouds that form at higher altitudes—1 to 3 miles (1.6 to 4.8 km) above the ground—are called *altocumulus* (*alto* means "high"). These clouds appear smaller than cumulus clouds, but this is simply because they are farther away.

As you sit still and look at cumulus clouds, you may see them grow into towering *cumulonimbus* clouds. Spotting such clouds is one way to predict the weather. *Nimb* means "rain," and the appearance of cumulonimbus clouds usually means that thunder, lightning, and rain are coming!

▲ Dense altostratus clouds cover the Sun.

TRY IT YOURSELF

Clouds form when water vapor condenses into liquid water droplets. You can watch this process by doing a simple experiment in your kitchen. Fill a metal ice cube tray with water and put it in the freezer. Allow the water to freeze completely.

Remove the ice cube tray and put it on a table. When you first take the tray out of the freezer, it is completely dry. In a few minutes, however, small drops of water will begin to form on the outside of the tray. The water drops form because the cold ice cube tray cools the air around it, causing water vapor in the air to condense.

▼ Umbrellas are good protection during a hail storm.

Stratus clouds are the dull, gloomy clouds you see on overcast days. Stratus clouds aren't puffy like cumulus clouds. Instead, they form in layers. Stratus clouds usually look dark because they block out the Sun—often they appear to cover the entire sky. When the skies begin to clear on an overcast day, it usually makes us happy to see the Sun creep out from behind a dark stratus cloud and create a bright, silvery edge. This explains the common expression, "Every cloud has a silver lining."

When stratus clouds form at an elevation of 1 to 3 miles (1.6 to 4.8 km) above the ground, they are called *altostratus* clouds. These clouds can also cover the entire sky.

One way to tell the difference between altostratus and stratus clouds is to look for the Sun. You won't be able to see it at all through a stratus cloud because the cloud is so dense. But through an altostratus cloud, the Sun will be barely visible—just a small circle of dull light. Another type of stratus cloud is one that produces rain or snow. This type is called *nimbostratus*.

Cirrus, the third main cloud type, means "curly" or "wispy." Cirrus clouds are found at least 3 miles (4.8 km) above the ground. Often they are much higher. Because temperatures at high altitudes are very low, cirrus clouds are made of ice crystals rather than water droplets. Cirrus clouds are very pretty, and they come in many different forms. Some cirrus clouds are white and feathery and look like horses' tails. Others are flat and layered like stratus clouds.

Layered cirrus clouds are called *cirrostratus* clouds. They usually fill the sky with milky-white color. A thin veil of cirrostratus clouds is often a good sign that rain is coming your way.

▲ Cirrus clouds are really floating ice crystals!

◀ San Francisco is a great place to see fog. Warm, humid air blowing off the Pacific Ocean passes over land, quickly cools, and forms millions and millions of cloud droplets. The thick fog often blocks the view of the Golden Gate Bridge.

Sometimes cirrus clouds form in patches or clumps. These clouds are called *cirrocumulus*, and they often resemble the scales of a fish, creating what skywatchers call a "mackerel sky."

There is another very common type of cloud that doesn't fit into any of the main categories: fog. Fog is nothing more than a cloud that forms at ground level. When it's foggy outside, you can literally "walk around with your head in the clouds."

Fog forms when air near the ground cools, causing water vapor to condense. Fog frequently forms in cool valleys and in coastal areas when winds blow warm, humid air over cool, dry land.

Rain and Snow

Let's see what happens, over a few weeks time, to a drop of water at the surface of the ocean. Like many others, our drop evaporates into the air and becomes invisible water vapor. The vapor is carried around with the wind until it is far from its previous home in the ocean. It travels up with the rising air, cools, condenses back into a water drop, and falls to the ground as rain. Once on the ground, the water drop rolls into a nearby river, which flows slowly but steadily toward the ocean. Finally, our drop comes back to the sea.

Precipitation, a word used to describe any kind of rain or snow, is something that many of us spend a lot of time thinking about: whether or not to wear a raincoat, whether the streets will be icy, whether there will be enough snow to cancel school. Precipitation occurs when water droplets floating within clouds combine and become so heavy that the air can no longer hold them.

Believe it or not, most precipitation begins as snow. The reason for this is that even in the summer, clouds can have temperatures

MAKE A RAINBOW

A rainbow is one of the most spectacular displays nature has to offer. Sunlight is a combination of violet, blue, green, yellow, orange, and red light. Seen together, the different colors of light look white. But when sunlight passes through a raindrop, the water acts like a prism— a glass that can split light into its separate colors. To see a rainbow, you have to be looking at the rain with the Sun behind you. You can only see a natural rainbow when the Sun is low in the sky.

You can create a rainbow in your own backyard. With your back to the Sun, use your garden hose to spray a fine mist in front of you. Does a rainbow appear in the water?

well below the freezing point, 32° F (0° C). This fact is easy to understand if you imagine that you are walking up the side of a tall mountain. The higher up you go, the colder the air becomes. Eventually you may even reach a point where there's snow on the ground.

At high elevations, clouds contain a lot of tiny ice crystals — formed from frozen water vapor. The ice crystals collect more water and get bigger and bigger until they are about the size of the tip of a toothpick. At this point, we stop calling them ice crystals and start calling them snowflakes. As the snowflakes fall toward the ground, they clump together with other snowflakes and grow even larger. If the temperature near the ground is high enough, the snowflakes melt and form raindrops.

Snowflakes form as tiny ice crystals fall out of a cloud. Some of the crystals stick to each other as they fall, creating unique designs. Some people say that no two snowflakes are exactly alike. Observe the beautiful shapes of snowflakes through a magnifying glass to see whether this is true.

There are several different types of rain. When raindrops are very small they're called *drizzle* or *mist*. Rain that starts and stops suddenly is called a *shower*. Rain that contains pollution is called **acid rain**, and it can be very destructive to plants, rivers, and lakes. Thunderstorms are often accompanied by *hail*, frozen clumps of raindrops that can be as large as 2 inches (5 centimeters) across. Large hailstones are very dangerous. Imagine how much damage might be caused by 2-inch chunks of ice falling from the sky!

Snow also comes in many different forms. Light snow falling for short periods of time is called *snow flurries* or *snow showers*. A severe storm, with drifting and blowing snow, is called a *blizzard*. Precipitation is sometimes a mix of both rain and snow. Some examples of mixed precipitation are *sleet*, *ice pellets*, and *freezing rain*.

During an ice storm, raindrops freeze *after* they hit the ground. Freezing rain creates an icy glaze that can break tree branches, snap power lines, and make driving treacherous.

▲ Digging out after a big snow

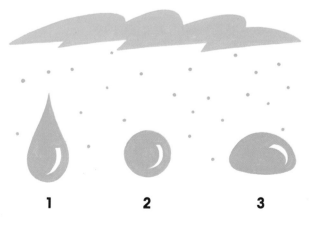

1 **2** **3**

◄ Which of these shapes looks the most like a raindrop? If you picked number 1, you are wrong! Small raindrops are shaped like a ball (number 2), because that's the form water vapor takes when it condenses. Large raindrops take on shape number 3, with a squashed bottom, because raindrops tend to flatten out as they fall.

3

WINDS AND WEATHER PATTERNS

Wind, a flowing current of air, is as familiar to us as night and day. Although we cannot see wind, we can feel it on a cold, blustery day and we can see leaves and branches blowing in the breeze. Let's examine the factors that cause the wind to blow.

As sunlight heats the Earth, certain areas get warmer than others. The tropics get quite hot, while the North and South poles remain cold. When air gets hot, it rises. When air gets cold, it sinks. Since warm air rises, it puts less pressure on the Earth than cold air does. Therefore we usually find low air pressure over warm areas, along the equator for instance, and high air pressure over cold areas, such as the North and South poles.

It is this contrast in pressure that causes wind, because air moves from high pressure to low pressure areas. You can see this yourself by using a balloon. As you blow air into the balloon, the pressure inside gets greater and greater. You create a contrast in pressure, with high pressure inside and low pressure outside the balloon. When you open up the balloon, the air rushes out, moving from the high pressure to the low pressure area. You've created wind!

HOT AIR RISES

Gas molecules are always moving around. In warm air, the molecules move quickly and expand, or spread out. In cold air, the molecules move more slowly and stay closer together. You can observe this difference by placing a balloon over the neck of an empty glass bottle. The balloon will droop over the side.

Now put the bottle in a pan of hot water. As the air inside the bottle gets warmer, the gas molecules move around faster and begin to expand. The expanding air will rise to fill up the balloon. Now remove the bottle from the pan. As the air inside the bottle cools, the molecules will slow down and contract, or move closer together. The balloon will droop down again.

◀ Hot-air ballooning

This movement of air from high to low pressure areas creates the great wind belts that surround the Earth. Near the equator are the *trade winds*, steady winds that flow from the northeast or southeast toward the equator. In past centuries, trading ships used these winds to cross the Atlantic Ocean. At the equator itself is the *intertropical convergence zone*, where the northern and southern trade winds meet. To the north and south we find the *horse latitudes*, calm zones with little or no wind. The name arises from the fact that sailors were often stranded in these zones and had to throw their horses overboard to lighten their load. North and south of the horse latitudes are the *prevailing westerlies*, where the wind usually blows from the west. Near the North and South poles we find the *polar easterlies*, with cold winds blowing from the east.

The Earth's prevailing wind systems owe their direction to a complex phenomenon known as the **Coriolis force**. The Coriolis force makes winds curve, because the Earth is spinning quickly beneath them.

The prevailing westerlies and easterlies account for the average wind conditions on Earth. But there are many other winds that affect specific areas. The *sea breeze* is a wind that flows from water toward land in coastal areas, often bringing relief on a hot summer afternoon. The *jet stream* is a swiftly flowing river of air several miles above the Earth's surface. The jet stream flows around the world from west to east, sometimes making large loops to the north and south. The jet stream can be as strong as 200 miles (322 km) per hour. This means that an airplane flight from New York to London, flying with the jet stream, is usually about an hour shorter than the return trip into the wind.

The Earth's Major Wind Systems

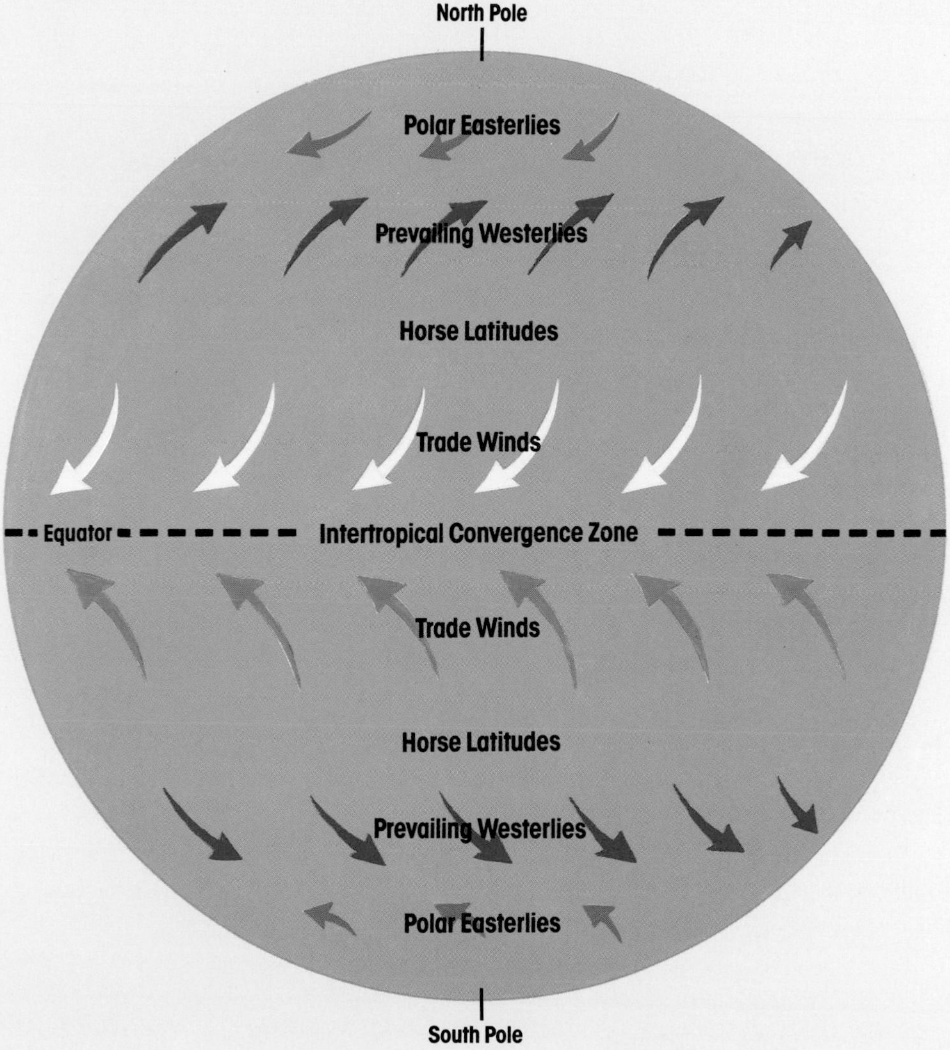

North Pole

Polar Easterlies

Prevailing Westerlies

Horse Latitudes

Trade Winds

Equator — Intertropical Convergence Zone

Trade Winds

Horse Latitudes

Prevailing Westerlies

Polar Easterlies

South Pole

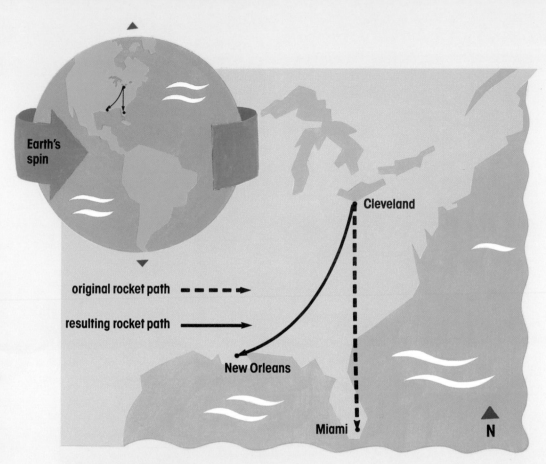

THE CORIOLIS FORCE

The Coriolis force makes the wind change direction. To understand how this force works, take a look at a map of the United States. Suppose you want to shoot a rocket from Cleveland, Ohio, to Miami, Florida.

You see on your map that Miami is almost due south of Cleveland, so you aim the rocket south and fire. Imagine your surprise the next day when you read in the paper that a rocket has hit New Orleans, Louisiana.

Even though your rocket was aimed due south, the Earth was spinning beneath it. By the time the rocket landed, the city of Miami had spun to the east, and your rocket landed far to the west. The wind works the same way. The Earth always spins beneath the wind, and this causes the wind to change its direction.

Some winds are predictable and others are constantly changing. Friction, the rubbing of air against hills, trees, and ocean waves, slows the wind down. Land masses, mountain ranges, and oceans can change the course of the wind. And air is constantly rising and sinking, responding to changes in air pressure and temperature. All these conditions cause the winds on Earth to shift, change, and circulate.

WINDCHILL FACTOR

In the winter, a strong wind makes cold temperatures feel even colder. For example, the actual temperature of the air may be 25° F (−4° C) one day, but, with a wind blowing at 20 miles (32 km) per hour, the air feels like it's −3° F (−20° C).

The difference in temperature occurs because the strong wind hitting your body causes you to lose heat more quickly than you would on a calm day. The colder temperature you feel is called the *windchill*. When the windchill factor is very low, it is important to wear plenty of warm clothes so you don't get frostbite when you go outside.

Pressure Systems

We have learned how air pressure, the weight of the atmosphere pressing down on Earth, creates wind. Air pressure is also responsible for much of our daily weather. If you look at a newspaper weather map on any given day, you will see that your region of the country might be covered by a high pressure system or by a low pressure system. Knowing whether your area is under a high or low pressure system will help you predict the kind of weather you might have.

A low pressure system is a huge mass of circulating air, with low pressure inside the system and high pressure on the outside. Because air moves from high pressure to low pressure areas, the air outside the system will spiral in toward the center, where the pressure is low, causing the air inside the system to rise. The rising air cools, and water vapor condenses, creating clouds and sometimes rain or snow.

A high pressure system is also a huge circulating air mass. It has high pressure on the inside and low pressure on the outside. In this system, the air in the center will sink and spiral toward lower pressure areas outside the system. Whereas rising air causes clouds and precipitation, sinking air leaves clear skies. High pressure systems, then, usually bring fair weather.

Radio and television weather forecasters usually report whether the **barometer** is rising or falling. The barometer is a scientific instrument that measures air pressure. If the barometer is rising, the pressure is getting higher, and you can bet the weather in your area will soon clear. When the barometer is falling, it means the pressure is getting lower, which will soon lead to rain, snow, or cloudy weather.

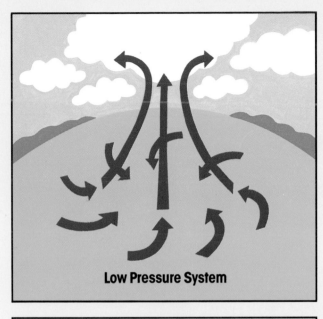

Low Pressure System

◄ Low and high pressure systems are huge spirals of air. Air under low pressure rises and cools, forming clouds and sometimes precipitation.

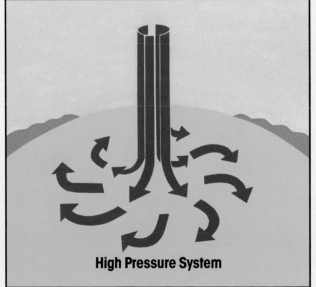

High Pressure System

◄ Air under high pressure sinks, leaving clear skies.

Today's forecast

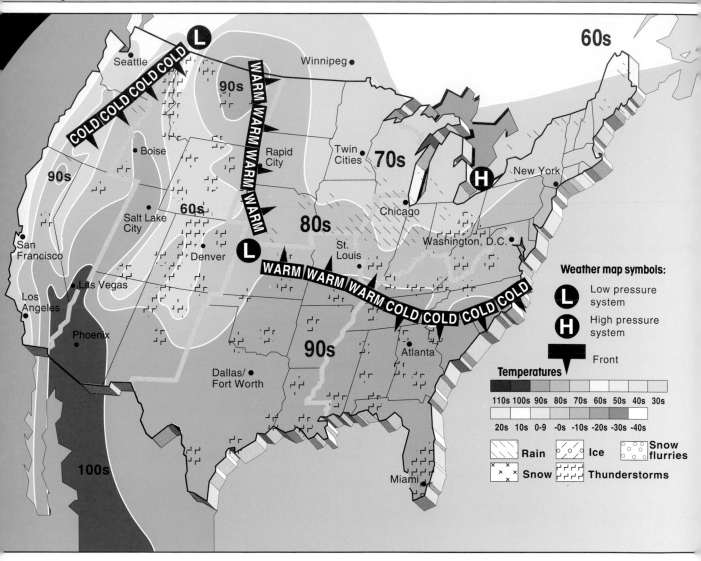

Courtesy of WeatherData Inc. and the *Minneapolis Star Tribune*

Fronts

Another weather feature that often shows up on weather maps is the **front.** A front is the border, or boundary, between warm and cold air. The two most common kinds of fronts are *warm fronts* and *cold fronts*.

A warm front forms when warm air, usually brought by winds from the south, bumps into cold air. When a warm front passes through your town, the temperature will rise.

Cold fronts form when cold air from the north bumps into warm air. A cold front passing through means that your region will soon get colder.

Most changes in the weather occur when fronts pass through. When warm and cold air bump into each other, wind directions change, and temperatures can change very quickly. It is not unusual for temperatures to rise or fall more than 15° F (8.5° C) when a front passes through.

Perhaps the most dramatic aspects of weather along fronts are clouds and precipitation. Since warm air rises and cold air sinks, warm air tends to rise up over cold air at a front. The rising air begins to cool, water vapor condenses, and clouds form. When the warm air rises very quickly, showers and thunderstorms form along fronts. In extreme cases, tornadoes sometimes form.

◄ Newspaper weather maps show precipitation, warm and cold fronts, areas of low and high pressure, and temperatures around the nation each day. Use the symbols on the map to find the weather forecast for your region.

4

STORMS

We have learned how water vapor creates clouds, rain, and snow and how moving air creates the wind and weather patterns all around us. Sometimes weather makes our lives difficult. The streets might be slippery with ice, humidity might make us uncomfortable, or cold air might whip through our clothing.

But some weather conditions are more than inconvenient. Storms are extreme disturbances that can cause great destruction.

Thunderstorms

A thunderstorm is one of the most fascinating and also one of the most dangerous aspects of the weather. Thunderstorms are likely to form in late afternoon or early evening on a hot summer day—although they can also form at other times. A thunderstorm not only brings heavy rain, thunder, and lightning, it can also bring hail, strong winds, and even tornadoes. Such storms, as you might recall, come from tall cumulonimbus clouds, or "thunderheads."

Thunderheads often measure more than 10 miles (16 km) from top to bottom. These dark clouds can grow to be as large as a

A giant cumulonimbus cloud
threatens thunder, lightning,
and heavy rains.

HAILSTONES

During severe thunderstorms, strong wind currents inside a cumulonimbus cloud can carry ice crystals up and down, again and again, between the top and the bottom of the cloud. The ice crystals grow bigger and bigger as they bump into liquid water droplets in the lower, warmer section of the cloud. When the ice crystals are swept back up to the higher, colder section of the cloud, they freeze into solid hailstones.

mountain, and may contain enough water to fill several large swimming pools.

If you've ever seen thunderheads grow large and dark before a storm, you know that such clouds are not calm collections of floating water drops. There is violent activity within the clouds. Air currents carry the water droplets up and down. The movement can be so fierce that the molecules inside the clouds become electrically charged. The electrical charges can build up and create lightning— a giant electrical spark.

A thunderstorm seen from afar

Lightning can travel inside a cloud, between a cloud and the ground, or between two clouds. The electricity inside a lightning bolt is awesome—enough to kill a person or an animal instantly. A lightning bolt heats the nearby air to a temperature of 54,000° F (30,200° C)—five times hotter than the surface of the Sun! The extreme heat causes molecules in the surrounding air to explode outward, creating a shock wave, or sonic boom. This boom is thunder—the sound of the heated air exploding.

Lightning is one of nature's most spectacular displays of power and beauty. Unfortunately, it is also one of the most deadly. Each year, more people are killed by lightning than by any other natural force. It's worth spending a few minutes to learn about lightning and how to avoid it—the knowledge might save your life one day.

There are many myths about lightning. The most famous is the belief that lightning can't strike the same place more than once. It can.

Lightning tends to strike isolated objects, such as a lone tree in a field. If you are caught in a thunderstorm, it isn't wise to stand under a tree. It is best to get inside a building. If you can't find shelter, stay away from trees and high places. Don't lie down, because if lightning strikes a short distance away, it can travel along the ground and reach you. Crouch down, keep your head as low as possible, and wait for the storm to pass.

You usually see lightning before you hear thunder because light travels almost a million times faster than sound. In fact, the sound of thunder takes about five seconds to travel one mile (about three seconds to travel one kilometer). You can use this knowledge to judge how far you are from a lightning stroke. Just count the number

◀ Lightning can be deadly.

LIGHTNING RODS

When lightning hits the ground, it tends to strike isolated, pointed objects like trees or tall buildings.

The lightning rod, a long metal spike attached to the roof of a building, is a safety device used to prevent lightning from damaging buildings and homes. Because the rod is tall and pointed, any lightning in the area is attracted to it.

When lightning strikes the lightning rod, the electricity travels harmlessly through a strong cable into the ground.

of seconds between the lightning flash and the sound of the thunder. Divide this number by five and you'll know the number of miles between you and the lightning (divide by three to find the distance in kilometers).

Tornadoes

Tornadoes, also called twisters or cyclones, are intense, swirling winds formed during severe thunderstorms. Tornadoes are some of the most destructive storms on Earth. Wind speeds in a tornado can reach 250 miles (402 km) per hour. These winds are strong enough to uproot trees and send entire houses flying through the air! Tornadoes usually last only a few minutes, but some have been reported to last for several hours. At ground level, most tornadoes are between 300 and 1,500 feet (91 to 457 m) across, while others can be more than a mile (1.6 km) wide.

A tornado usually forms from upward-moving winds, or updrafts, inside a cumulonimbus cloud. If these winds start to rotate, they will form a "funnel cloud," a swirling wind that snakes downward from the base of the thunderhead. When the funnel reaches the ground, it becomes a tornado and kicks up a lot of dirt and debris. This flying debris can cause a lot of damage, especially when it includes objects as large as trees and automobiles!

Most of the world's tornadoes occur in the central United States. In the area called Tornado Alley, which stretches from central Texas through Nebraska, over 200 tornadoes occur each year. This area is especially likely to have tornadoes because this is where cold air from Canada frequently meets warm air from the Gulf of Mexico, creating severe thunderstorms. Most tornadoes occur in late afternoon between March and July, although tornadoes have occurred during every month of the year.

If a tornado is likely to form in your area, radio and television stations will report that a government agency called the National Weather Service has issued a "tornado watch." This means that

A funnel cloud churns across the prairie.

tornadoes are possible. If a "tornado warning" is issued, it means a tornado has been spotted, either by observers or on a radar screen, and you should take cover. The safest place to be during a tornado is in a basement or an underground shelter.

Hurricanes

Another type of storm with fierce, swirling winds is the hurricane. Hurricanes often form over the North Atlantic Ocean and parts of the Pacific. Hurricanes also occur in other parts of the world, but they have different names, like "willy-willy" in Australia, "typhoon" in India, and "baguio" in the Philippines.

A hurricane will develop over warm ocean waters in the tropics when individual thunderstorms join together to form clusters. When such a storm begins, we call it a *tropical disturbance*. If it intensifies, it becomes a *tropical depression*, and then a *tropical storm*. Only when the winds are stronger than 74 miles per hour (119 km/h) is the storm called a hurricane.

Hurricane winds batter the coast.

This photograph, taken from a space shuttle, shows a hurricane's circular shape and the calm "eye" at the center of the storm.

Hurricanes may be hundreds of miles across. They have a circular shape, with intense winds and long bands of clouds spiraling in toward the center. In the middle of the hurricane is the *eye*, a calm area with clear skies.

People who live along the Gulf of Mexico, near the Atlantic coast of the United States, or on the Caribbean Islands are well aware of the damage that a hurricane can cause. The biggest problems occur while the hurricane is still well out at sea. The storm creates high waves that can flood coastal areas. When the hurricane hits the coast, high winds and blinding rains can wipe out entire towns. To make matters worse, many hurricanes cause tornadoes after they reach land! Fortunately, hurricanes weaken and eventually fizzle out after they hit the coast.

The National Weather Service issues a "hurricane watch" when a hurricane threatens to pass over a particular area. When it appears that the storm will strike the area within 24 hours, a "hurricane warning" is issued. This warning is designed to give people who live in the path of a hurricane enough time to leave their homes and travel to a safe place.

5

WEATHER
FORECASTING

Imagine a weather forecaster in a large city. It is his or her responsibility to forecast the weather accurately so that thousands or even millions of people know if they should expect a major winter storm, wear a raincoat, or put on an extra sweater. That sounds like a tough job, especially when you consider how irritated people can become when the forecast is incorrect.

In the old days, weather wisdom was largely based on folklore and superstition. People relied on sayings like "ring around the moon, rain will come soon" to predict the next day's weather. This approach to weather forecasting was fun and easy to learn, but, unfortunately, it wasn't very accurate.

The science of meteorology has improved by leaps and bounds in the last century, but we are still unable to predict the weather with perfect accuracy. Take a look out the window and you'll notice how random the weather seems to be. One minute the trees may be swaying in a gentle breeze, the next minute they might be standing completely still. A passing cloud could bring shade and cooler temperatures, and perhaps a brief shower. Sunny skies and warmer

The weather vane is a simple tool that makes it easy to tell which way the wind is blowing.

temperatures might follow. These and other random weather features are impossible to predict with complete accuracy. But meteorologists do have many tools that help them "predict the unpredictable."

The first step in making a weather forecast is to determine, as thoroughly as possible, the present weather conditions over a large area. There are thousands of observation stations in the United States that give hourly reports to the National Weather Service on temperature, humidity, pressure, and wind speed and direction. More than 100 of these stations take twice-daily measurements of atmospheric conditions using **radiosondes**, packages of weather instruments that are carried many miles above the ground by weather balloons. Satellites orbiting above the Earth can photograph clouds and storms from hundreds of miles in the air. Radar stations gather additional weather information.

A scientist from the National Center for Atmospheric Research works at a portable weather station. The station has equipment for measuring wind speed, air pressure, temperature, humidity, and rainfall.

When all available information has been collected, the forecaster prepares charts and maps, drawn both by hand and by computer, to summarize the present weather conditions in his or her area.

The second step in making a weather forecast is to use a computer to predict how the existing weather conditions will change. Meteorologists at the National Weather Service have designed computer programs and elaborate mathematical formulas that help people examine a wide range of weather conditions.

These programs enable forecasters to analyze existing weather conditions and predict when and where it will rain or snow, what temperatures to expect, the likely wind speed and direction, and what types of clouds might form over a large area.

The final step in weather forecasting is the most important one. Each meteorologist must study the existing weather and use his or her experience to make the best possible forecast decision. This is also called the "human factor," or the art of weather forecasting.

Certain weather patterns are very easy to predict. For instance, when warm, moist air flows over a tall mountain, the air is sure to rise and then cool. Meteorologists know that this situation will almost certainly bring clouds and precipitation.

But other weather conditions are more difficult to predict, and

WEATHER RADAR

Radar is an important weather-forecasting tool. Radar transmitters send out signals that bounce off ice crystals and water droplets in clouds. By studying the returning signals, meteorologists know the size and location of approaching storms.

On the radar screen at right, the yellow and red areas indicate thunderstorms.

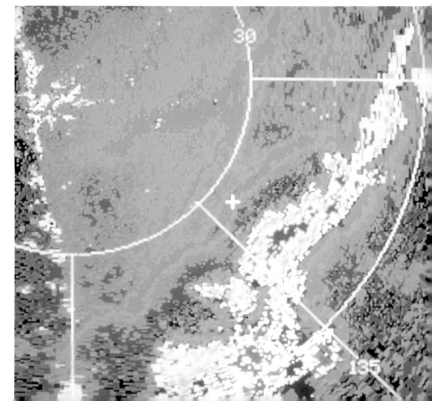

the forecaster's experience becomes even more important. A computer program can't predict exactly when the afternoon sea breeze will begin to cool things off in a coastal area. So the forecaster must rely on nearby weather observations as well as his or her own skill and experience to make an accurate prediction.

Suppose a winter storm is approaching your area. The forecaster might recall a similar storm a few years earlier that brought a major snowfall. By comparing the current conditions to those of the previous storm, the forecaster can figure out how much snow to expect.

Computer programs cannot do everything. Experience is one of the weather forecaster's most important tools.

These long-distance runners are dressed for the weather.

Whatever the case may be, forecasters must consider all available information, including their own experience, and make the best possible prediction. More often than not, they're right!

We've already come a long way from being "otherwise" toward our goal of being "weatherwise." It's nice to understand something about a popular topic of conversation. So the next time someone says, "Nice day, isn't it?" we'll know what we're talking about when we answer, "It sure is."

GLOSSARY

acid rain: rain that contains sulfuric acid, nitric acid, or other pollutants

air pressure: the weight of the atmosphere pressing down on the Earth

atmosphere: the layer of gases surrounding the Earth

axis: an imaginary line from the North Pole to the South Pole, straight through the center of the Earth

barometer: a meteorological instrument that measures air pressure

climate: the most typical weather that occurs in a particular region of the Earth

condensation: the process by which water vapor cools and forms liquid water

condensation nuclei: tiny particles of dust, smoke, and salt. Water vapor condenses around these particles and forms water droplets in clouds.

Coriolis force: a force that makes the wind change direction, due to the spinning of the Earth

evaporation: the process by which liquid water changes to a gas

front: a boundary between warm and cold air

humidity: the amount of water vapor in the air

meteorologist: a scientist who studies and predicts the weather

molecule: the smallest particle into which a substance, such as oxygen, can be divided

precipitation: any kind of rain or snow, such as drizzle, sleet, hail, or snow flurries

radiosonde: a package of meteorological instruments attached to a balloon. The instruments measure pressure, wind speed, wind direction, temperature, and humidity at different locations above the ground.

revolution: the circular motion of the Earth around the Sun. This motion determines the changing seasons on Earth.

rotation: the circular motion of the Earth on its axis. This motion is responsible for the difference between day and night.

ultraviolet radiation: energy coming from the Sun that can harm plants and animals. Ultraviolet radiation is absorbed by ozone in the atmosphere.

water cycle: the movement of water from the oceans to the atmosphere (through evaporation), from the atmosphere to the Earth (in the form of rain and snow), and from the land to the oceans (by way of streams and rivers)

water vapor: water in gas form. Water vapor is created when liquid water evaporates.

INDEX

Sailors know that winds can be unpredictable. Winds might suddenly shift, increase, or die down.

ACKNOWLEDGMENTS

Photographs and illustrations courtesy of Mike Magnuson, p. 2; Michael Mogil, pp. 7, 20, 23, 25, 26 (both), 28 (bottom), 30, 32, 43, 45, 46, 55; United States Department of Agriculture, p. 9; Liz Monson, pp. 10, 19, 21, 33 (bottom), 37, 38, 41; Maine Office of Tourism, p. 11; Experimental Aircraft Association, p. 12; Ruth Karl, p. 13; Emily Slowinski, p. 14; Bachman's Garden Center, p. 15; National Center for Atmospheric Research, pp. 16, 28 (top), 31, 47, 51, 56, 57, 64; Toro Corporation, p. 33 (top); Lynda Richards, p. 35; Tim Steinberg, p. 39; WeatherData, Inc. and *Minneapolis Star Tribune*, p. 42; Thomas O. Reese, p. 49; Visuals Unlimited, p. 52; National Aeronautics and Space Administration, p. 53; Jerome Rogers, p. 58; Benjamin Brink, p. 59; John Mallitte, p. 63; Craig Blouin, front cover.